✱ WHAT'S THEIR STORY? ✱

Roald Dahl

Oxford University Press, Great Clarendon Street, Oxford OX2 6DP

Oxford New York Athens Auckland Bangkok
Bogotá Buenos Aires Calcutta Cape Town Chennai Dar es Salaam
Delhi Florence Hong Kong Istanbul Karachi Kuala Lumpur
Madrid Melbourne Mexico City Mumbai Nairobi Paris
São Paulo Singapore Taipei Tokyo Toronto Warsaw
and associated companies in Berlin Ibadan

Oxford is a registered trade mark of Oxford University Press
Text © Andrea Shavick 1997
Illustrations © Oxford University Press 1997

First published 1997

British Library Cataloguing in Publication Data. Data available

ISBN 0–19–910434–4 (hardback)
ISBN 0–19–910440–9 (paperback)
ISBN 0–19–918654–5 (Branch Library Pack B)

5–7–9–10–8–6–4

Printed in Hong Kong

Roald Dahl

THE CHAMPION STORYTELLER

ANDREA SHAVICK

Illustrated by Alan Marks

OXFORD UNIVERSITY PRESS

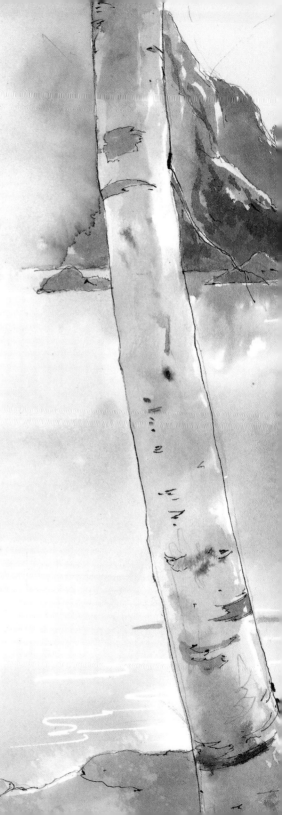

Today Roald Dahl is known as a famous children's author. But during his life he was also a boxing champion and a fighter pilot, and he invented a machine that saved thousands of children's lives.

Roald was born in 1916 in Cardiff, Wales. He lived with his Norwegian parents, one brother and four sisters in a grand house with acres of farmland. Every summer the whole family travelled to Norway to visit Roald's grandparents. While the rest of the family went out in their boat, Roald sat on his grandmother's lap, listening to her wonderful stories about witches and giants and magic. He was spellbound.

When Roald was only three years old, two very sad events happened. His sister Astri became very ill and died. Then three weeks later, his father also died. Little Roald felt terribly sad and lonely.

By the age of six, Roald was already a bit of a daredevil. Instead of simply walking to school, he liked to hurtle along on a tricycle right down the middle of the road!

He was also always up to mischief. One day he decided to play a trick on the owner of the local sweet shop. All the children called her a witch because she had long, dirty fingernails and a cross, witch's voice. While his friends kept her busy, Roald slipped a dead mouse into one of her jars of sweets. But somehow she discovered who had played the trick and told his headmaster. Roald's punishment was a terrible beating. When his mother saw the bruises she vowed never to send him back to that school again.

But Roald had to go to school somewhere.

Roald was sent to boarding school in England. Desperately homesick, he lay on his bed groaning and clutching his stomach, pretending to be ill. It worked! The school matron sent him home. Unfortunately, he could not fool his own doctor, who sent him straight back to school again.

Even during the holidays Roald could not keep out of trouble. One day his oldest sister took the whole family for a ride in their new car. From the back seat Roald shouted at her to go faster and faster, and she did. She drove so fast that the car spun out of control and crashed. Roald was thrown through the windscreen and landed in a ditch. His nose was almost sliced off.

Somehow, his mother managed to hold his nose in place with a handkerchief until they got home. Poor Roald had to lie on the table while the doctor sewed it back on.

At Roald's school there was a lot of bullying. Every day during the winter, one of the older boys made Roald sit on a freezing toilet seat to warm it up for him! And children were often beaten by their teachers just for making mistakes or talking in class. Roald thought it was very unfair. Why should bullies get away with it, he thought? Why should teachers be allowed to hurt pupils?

Luckily, not everything at school was bad. Once a term Cadbury's, the chocolate makers, sent every pupil a large box of chocolate bars. They wanted to find out which of their new chocolates the children liked best. Roald loved tasting all these new chocolates and spent ages deciding which were his favourites. Many years later he remembered this when he was writing his famous book, *Charlie and the Chocolate Factory.*

Another part of school life that Roald really loved was sport. He played cricket, golf, football and hockey, and was the captain of the squash team. But when he decided to enter the boxing championship, Roald's friends tried desperately to stop him. He had never boxed before, and they thought he would get badly hurt. However, Roald was determined to go ahead.

As he stepped into the boxing ring, Roald's friends held their breath. The two boxers jabbed at each other a few times, circling around. Then, like a flash of lightning, Roald gave his opponent an almighty punch. The other boxer was out cold. Roald had won! He went on to win the whole championship.

When Roald reached the age of eighteen it was time to leave school for ever. Other boys were going on to university, but Roald wanted to travel. He longed to go somewhere exciting, and as far away from England as possible.

Roald decided that the best way for him to travel was to work for a company in a different country. He joined Shell Oil in Africa, delivering the oil that kept the machines in the diamond mines working. To get to the mines he had to drive through the African countryside, past herds of wild animals. Roald loved seeing all the elephants, giraffes, lions and zebras, but there was one animal he was terribly afraid of – the deadly poisonous Mamba snake.

In 1939, when Roald was twenty-three, the Second World War began. Longing for more excitement, he joined the Royal Air Force straight away. He had always wanted to learn to fly, and now he would be paid to learn! One day he was told to fly out to join 80 Squadron in the Libyan desert, in north Africa. Roald studied the map so he would know exactly where to find them. But the map was wrong.

Roald took off in his little plane with the map tied to his leg. When he reached the spot marked on the map he looked for 80 Squadron. But they were nowhere to be seen. And the plane was nearly out of fuel! Roald knew he had to land. As the plane touched down, it hit a rock and the petrol tank exploded.

The roar from the explosion was deafening. For several moments Roald was too shocked to move. Then he felt an unbearable stinging heat as his clothes caught fire and his skin started to burn.

Somehow, Roald managed to roll out of the plane and crawl away. Miraculously, some British soldiers saw the plane crash. They found Roald lying unconscious on the ground and rushed him to hospital.

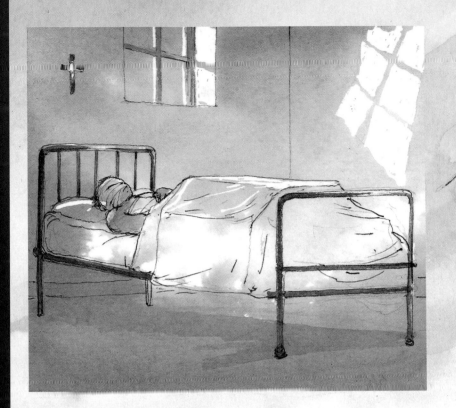

When Roald woke up his whole body was covered in bandages. His legs were broken, his hips and back were damaged and his nose had been totally smashed. But he was much more worried about his sight. His face was so bruised he could not open his eyes. It was a long road to recovery.

At last Roald was well enough to leave hospital. He was supposed to go home, but he was determined to fly again. He rejoined his RAF fighter squadron, and fought bravely in many air battles over Greece and the Middle East. Roald was a real war hero.

In the end, however, he became ill with painful headaches whenever he flew. Roald's flying days were over, but a new adventure was just beginning.

In 1942 the RAF offered Roald a new job in Washington, USA as an assistant at the British Embassy. One of his first tasks was to write an account of what it was like to be a fighter pilot in the war. To his amazement, a leading newspaper offered him a thousand dollars for his very first story, 'Shot Down Over Libya'. Once it was published, other newspapers all over the United States wanted his stories. Roald quickly became a successful and famous writer.

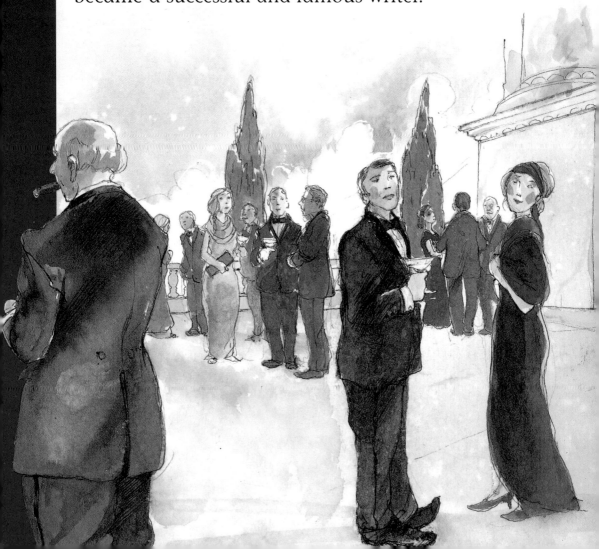

Roald loved being famous. He loved the way everyone wanted to know him, even people like Walt Disney and the President of the United States. One day he was introduced to a beautiful actress called Patricia Neal. For the first time in his life, Roald fell deeply in love, and before long he was engaged to be married.

After they were married, Pat and Roald bought a house just outside London. At the bottom of the garden stood a small hut. As soon as he set eyes on it, Roald knew it would be the perfect place to write.

It was not long before baby Olivia was born. Then came Tessa, and then Theo. The children looked forward to bedtime, when Roald would tell them one of his made-up stories. Their favourite one was about a lonely little orphan boy called James, who hides in an enormous magical peach to escape from his wicked aunts. Another story they loved was about a little boy called Charlie, who is taken on a tour of an incredible chocolate factory owned by Willy Wonka. These bedtime stories later became Roald's first full-length children's books: *James and the Giant Peach* and *Charlie and the Chocolate Factory*.

One day, while the whole family were staying in New York, something terrible happened. Roald's baby son, Theo, was being taken for a walk in his pram by the nanny, when suddenly a taxi hurtled round the corner. It smashed into Theo's pram, and broke some of the bones in his head.

Theo was very badly injured, but Roald was determined not to let him die. Together with a doctor called Kenneth Till, and an engineer called Stanley Wade, Roald invented a special machine to remove the fluid that was collecting in Theo's brain. Theo recovered, and the machine saved the lives of thousands of other children as well.

Two years later, the poor Dahl family was hit by another tragedy. In those days children were not protected so well against disease as they are today, and Roald's daughter, Olivia, died suddenly from measles.

Roald was heartbroken. He locked himself in the hut at the bottom of the garden and concentrated on his writing. It was the only thing that could help him forget what had happened, for a little while at least. Even when the weather was bitterly cold he still worked on, snuggled up in a sleeping bag to keep warm. He sat in an old armchair, surrounded by pencils and chocolate bars, filling dozens of exercise books with his extremely messy handwriting. He wanted his stories to be perfect, so he sometimes wrote out the same page hundreds of times before he was satisfied with it.

Having worked so hard on his stories, Roald was desperate to find a British publisher for them. Every one he contacted said his stories were too rude, and too scary for children. But Roald was crafty. He asked his daughter, Tessa, to give copies of *Charlie* and *James* to her friend Camilla Unwin, whose father was a publisher. Mr Unwin liked the stories so much he agreed to publish them.

The following years brought Roald enormous success. So many people bought his books, he became a millionaire. But there were disappointments too. When Roald saw the film of his book, *The Witches*, he was furious because the film-makers had completely changed the ending without asking his permission.

Roald often made his characters seem realistic by basing them on people he actually knew. The bullies and cruel teachers he remembered from his schooldays appeared in the shape of evil giants, wicked witches, grumpy grannies and horrid headmistresses. Roald enjoyed giving them all a delightfully sticky end. Lots of details in Roald's stories came from real life, too. The Big Friendly Giant walked up a road that looked exactly like his local high street, and Danny, the champion of the world, lived in a caravan just like the one Roald's own children used as a playhouse when they were younger.

As he grew older, Roald developed a reputation for behaving badly. He would often upset people by making fun of them or being rude. He also delighted in doing unexpected things, like popping into schools and surprising all the children. More than anything, he wanted to write stories that were so funny and so exciting, children would fall in love with them – and he succeeded.

Roald died in 1990 aged 74, having become one of the most successful and popular children's authors of all time. His incredibly funny, rude and amazing stories have been translated into many languages. Millions of children all over the world have read and enjoyed his books. Millions more will read and enjoy them in the future.

Important dates in Roald Dahl's life

1916 Born in Cardiff, Wales
1925 Sent to school in England
1938 Goes to work in Africa with Shell Oil
1939 Joins Royal Air Force and trains as fighter pilot
1940 Plane crash in Libya
1942 Works in Washington, USA. Starts writing
1953 Marries actress Patricia Neal
1955–1965 Has five children
1960 Son Theo has tragic accident
1961 Roald's first book for children, *James and the Giant Peach*, is published
1962 Daughter Olivia dies
1964 *Charlie and the Chocolate Factory* is published
1961–1990 Writes many bestselling books, including *The Twits*, *The BFG*, *The Witches* and *Matilda*
1990 Dies in Oxford, England, aged 74

Index